MEDITATIONS ON BEING

meditations on being

//

Rachel Fox

Foreword by Benjamin W. Decker

Illustrations by
Kelsey Anne Heimerman

La
Reunion

DALLAS, TEXAS

La

Reunion

La Reunion Publishing, an imprint of Deep Vellum
3000 Commerce St., Dallas, Texas 75226

deepvellum.org · @deepvellum

Deep Vellum is a 501c3 nonprofit literary arts organization
founded in 2013 with the mission to bring the world into
conversation through literature.

978-1-64605-037-6 (paperback)
978-1-64605-038-3 (ebook)

Support for this publication has been provided in part by
grants from the National Endowment for the Arts,
the Texas Commission on the Arts,
the City of Dallas Office of Arts and Culture's ArtsActivate program,
and the Moody Fund for the Arts:

LIBRARY OF CONGRESS CONTROL NUMBER: 2020945925

Front cover design © 2020
by Kelsey Anne Heimerman | kelseyanneheimerman.com
Interior Layout and Typeset by KGT

This book is gratefully dedicated to my family, friends, and all those who love me—thank you for that incomparable gift.

It is with you in mind and heart that I write these words; you animate me.

Foreword

Poetry has a way of reaching into the mind and soul with a magic and power proportionate to the reader's availability and openness to it. We take for granted the supernatural possibilities of the spoken and written word in our more utilitarian daily use thereof. Rather than instructing someone in exactly what technique with which to approach a task, poetry calls for subtle resonance, like a melodic invitation to intimacy with an experience. In poetry, we find the difference between indoctrination and art.

Of course, we live in a world where the "scientifically proven benefits" of meditation fill headlines as the masses rush to know exactly how to use meditation to stay young, relieve anxiety, and sleep better. Rachel Fox takes a step down a road long ignored by the benefit-seekers of today: vulnerable existential contemplation. While there are no doubt plenty more benefits to a meditation practice than mentioned here, it should be stated that the evolutionary potential of the individual is unlocked through an exploration of one's consciousness. *Meditations on Being* invites the modern reader into a sometimes simple, and other times profoundly nuanced, reflection on what it means to live in a living universe.

Our interconnectedness with the world that surrounds us and all others who have lived and will live cannot be taught; it must be realized. And so, in the great faith traditions of all cultures across the globe, we find poetry, parables, fables, and myths, designed to lead the student toward that realization. The archetypal messages of these things reveal more than meets the conscious mind, and the deeper the pondering, the more potential for genuine transformation. These great moments of enlightening realization lead and guide us on the path ordained specifically for us, and the same poem will be understood a thousand ways when exposed to a thousand minds.

As you read Rachel Fox's *Meditations on Being*, take your time. Breathe as you read. Observe your mind and your heart as the messages move and change you. Poetry is not a book to be completed, a task to be checked off a list, or a triumph to declare—but a relationship to be cultivated, and, ultimately, the relationship is with oneself and the sublime. Our world is in desperate need of truth-seekers who establish a firm foundation of psychological sanity and emotional stability while boldly reaching into the infinite with the mind. You are among those earnestly sought and prayed for truth-seekers, and we are grateful you are here. May the magic inside this book deepen your connection to the great beyond, and may you live more fully from that place.

Benjamin W. Decker
Author, *Modern Spirituality*

meditations on being

on action //

as
i move
i know
i am.

on action ii //

as it
moves
through
my form
it is true—

i am
everything
i do.

on adversity //

to suffer
much is
to know
you can.

on aging //

it isn't
too late
to do
something
great.

on analog //

real life
has a
totally
touchable
interface.

on analog ii //

there is nothing
like the warmth
of a person

in person.

on anatomy //

it would
not seem
divine
mistake

that woman,

on her
own,

can
her own
pleasure
make.

on apathy //

no one
cries
a tear
for the
fly in
their glass
of wine.

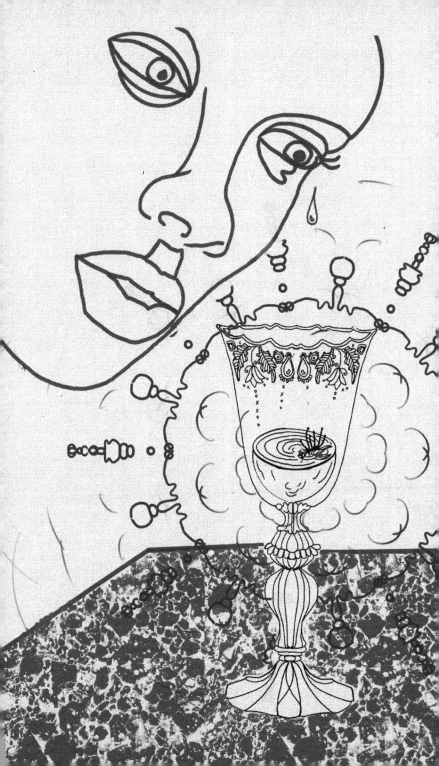

on art //

as we
make
our
dreams
concrete,

the bits
of
marble
left over
weep.

as scraps
fall
wisely
at our
feet,

and bow
to the
genius
of
artistry.

on art ii //

love knows
no language
better than
the one
you speak
it in.

on attachment //

what if
we let go
of what
this needed
to be?

on babel //

of all
the true love
ever
made,

how much
was not
truly
lost in
translation?

unrequited—

this love
mimics
its own
creation.

and the
true love
truly
sent and
received?

we call this
communication–

true love's
creative
liberation.

on balance //

she was
firm and
soft in
all the
right
places.

on beginning //

a seed
planted
only
knows
one way

.   .   .

out.

on being //

i feel
so alive,

i can
not be
contained.

i open
now revived,

i can
not be
restrained.

i find
such delight,

i can
not be
detained.

i am
so divine,

i can
not be
explained.

on being ii //

i am!
i am all.
i am all alone.
i am all alone here.

i wish!
i wish you.
i wish you were.
i wish you were here.

here i am.
here i am all.
here i am all alone.
here i am all alone wishing.
here i am all alone wishing you.
here i am all alone wishing you
were.
here i am all alone wishing you
were here.

here
i am!

on being iii //

closed eyes have faith
in their ability to
reopen;
cut off the beauty
embrace the
blackness
trust that goodness
will choose
to remain. with
love for light
and hope for darkness
there lies
sense in
every madness. quell
the exultant dove
and she will
sing again.

on between //

to embrace
the next
moment,
we must
let go
of this one.

on blame //

the
finger
you point
begins
with
your hand.

on boundaries //

i do not
owe you
access
to myself.

on brother //

he is
the joyful one
the rising son
the curse undone

the everyone.

he is
just in time
just a sign
just divine

just design.

he is
one who aids
one who braves
one who displays

one who saves.

he is the
brother who stays.

on business //

when
creativity
is currency,
you are
your own mint.

on care //

a loving
attention
is medicine.

on character //

strength is not
by accident.

on charity //

time is
a gift
when it comes
unwrapped,
without
strings.

on charity ii //

do the
good right
in front
of you.

on clarity //

the point
is simply
taken when
simply put.

on collaboration //

and all
the world
is a
loom
for those
who seek
to weave
together.

on commitment //

for some
reason,

when your
time spent

is your
time lent,

labor
seems a
shorter
season.

on commitment ii //

give it
everything
you think
you have,

and you
will find
so much
more there.

on complaint //

your bad
mood does
not look
better on
anyone
else.

on complaint ii //

dissatisfaction
with creation
is madness.

on confidence //

how
about
you take
just one
step off
of the
cliff?

falling

smiling

flying

past
rushing
whispers
of

'what if?'

on confidence ii //

play with
your own
idea of
who you are—

y o u
stretches
far.

on confidence iii //

humility
wears well
in all weather.

on confidence iv //

maybe
you doubt
your doubts
today?

on consumption //

i am
a sacred
container
for what
i fill
myself
with.

on control //

the desire
to fix
is what
needs
fixing.

on convenience //

the fruit
low on
the tree
is just
easiest
to see.

on creativity //

i can
only
imagine
what
we will
imagine
next.

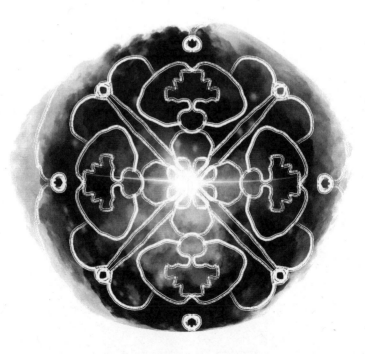

on criticism //

your words
are the stones
i sharpen
the blade of
myself upon.

on criticism ii //

doubts feast
on failures
perceived.

on cultivation //

plant seeds
of pain
and see
a sorry
harvest.

on dating //

i thought
you might be
a great love
of my life,

but
here we are

and it seems

you are just
a good love
for tonight.

on dating ii //

perhaps
a crush
is most like
an itch,
of all things?

on darkness //

and when
i reached
the place
where light
had not
been,

i found
a poem
there.

on decision //

let it
marinate;

the truth
holds its
flavor well.

on deluge //

if words
came like
the flood
of sense,
i would
make more.

on desire //

why is it
when we see
a light,
we want to
dim it?

why is it
when we see
a prize,
we want to
win it?

why oh why
is possession
a mental
limit?

if you love it,
you do not
own it,
you live it.

on direction //

why would
you find
your way
before
you lost it?

on discovery //

how could
we arrive
at the nature
of the universe,

if we keep
running
from the nature
of ourselves?

on display //

if i let
me feel
i can
move you.

on doubt //

nothing
kills
a dream
quite like
you do.

on duality //

if i
were to
look into
your eyes
looking
into mine;

−two points
one line−

who would
be receiving
the attention

as our
sights align?

on duality ii //

the warmth
between us;
a whole
from
two parts.

on duality iii //

alone
i am,

but us,
we are
together.

on duality iv //

she was
herself
both an
artist
and a
work of
art.

on education //

want to
know something?

know thyself.

on ego //

let go
and you
cannot
be owned.

on emotion //

love and
pain do
beget
themselves.

on empty //

every
true love
leaves a
void in
its wake.

on endings //

it doesn't
have to
work out,

and you
don't have
to mind.

on endings ii //

the end
of a thing
is bitter
and sweet
all at once.

on entropy //

harmony
returns
only to
again
disperse.

on evolution //

we are
made to
improve.

on evolution ii //

i thought i knew
who i really was,

and then i took
another breath.

another birth;
another death.

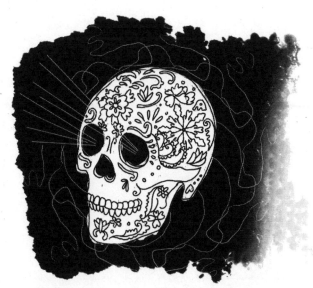

ANOTHER BIrth/ANOTHer DEAth./ON evolution ii

on example //

because
you do not
see it
around you,

does not
make it
beyond you.

on excuses //

you will
count the
reasons
why not
until you
run out

of time

or reasons.

on experience //

when it
comes to
sensations,

don't play
favorites.

on experience ii //

no matter
what it meant
to you then,

it always
meant something.

on exposure //

if anyone
is going
to see you,

you have to
reveal
yourself.

on exposure ii //

no one
could speak
your truth
quite like
you do.

on faith //

i met god
one day
inside of
my mind,

at the door
somewhere

between
hello and
goodbye;

it seemed
like forever,

and the blink
of an eye.

on faith ii //

everything
arises and
arrives
right on time.

on fantasy //

i met
my desire
once,

on the steps.

she was
dressed
nice,

and we spoke.

i could
have stayed
there

all night long.

on fantasy ii //

your body
is on my mind,

and i am
definitely
not asking it
to get off.

on fate //

eternity
is decided
by each of us
every day.

on favorites //

when my
preferences
saw clearly,

they were
subjects of
their own
tyranny,

most of them
parted ways.

on fear //

be brave;

it's your
heart you
will save.

on forgiveness //

the very
place you
hurt me,

i love
you there.

on form //

like the
sun of
dawn,

our
silhouettes
are so
divinely
drawn.

on friends //

my heart is
wherever
in the world
you are.

on friends ii //

if i made
a wish
it would
sound like
talking
to you.

on gathering //

alchemy
is a
present
moment
event !

on gender //

yang
opened
his eyes
and they
filled
with yin.

he drank
her in.

she
loved
him right
then deep
within.

on genesis //

to desire
and be desired in
return.
to life
before knowledge
before the creation
of this idea
beautiful inside our
heads. touch
with closest
breaths and
sweetest skin
tingles pure
for every
kiss. against
the time and
place, dangled like
a mangled plane
crashed in the tree
of life,
before it grew
tall with
knowledge,
and the creation
of this.

on genesis ii //

some things
must be
perfect
in what
they are;

love is
one of
those.

on gifts //

if you
gave me
one thing,

let it
be your
best love.

on god //

for him,

she put
pen to page;

love expressed
at every stage.

on god ii //

my body
may be my
own refuge,

my heart
may hold my
own resolve,

but i am
the lord's

first and
foremost;

everything
i am is
his love.

on grace //

my hopes
have risen
to meet
challenge
to them.

on grief //

what sound
does a
heart make
when it
breaks?

on growth //

i see
the future;
in fracture,
a seed.

on happiness //

gladness
does not
begin at
the tips of
receiving
fingers,

but rather
the bottom
of a
grateful heart.

on hardship //

your trouble
is your
teacher in
kid clothes.

on healing //

the honey
that flows
from the
wound in
the tree
is sweet.

on hope //

i put
my seed
of love
into
the earth,
and it
grew tall
and strong.

on hope ii //

you will
find me
in the
smallest
places,

in the
darkest
corners,

for i am
the light
at the
bottom
of the ocean,

i am
the heat
at the
center
of the earth;

i am life
i am life
i am life.

on humanity //

and god
forgave
them all
without
question.

on humanity ii //

it is
bright,
this place,

when we
open
our eyes;

the sun,
fresh
new pain–

our first
breath of
alive.

then hurt
and alone,

we toss
pain to
and fro.

so woe

comes
and goes,

like love
ebbs
and flows.

on humility //

when the
divine
entered,
his presence
was humbly
unannounced.

on identity //

everybody
will be
somebody
if they
let them
happen.

on image //

what is
the purpose
of a
photograph
but to
capture
the light?

on imagination //

how
would
you
materialize it,

before
you
could
visualize it?

on immortality //

magic
is made
when the
minds
of many
move as
one;

this is
how
the real
alchemy
is done.

on impossibility //

before you
sense it,

often
it makes
no sense.

so be
porous
to the new,

not dense.

on improvement //

better
is your
next best.

on inability //

is it

can't
or
won't?

i cannot
and
will not
decide.

on inability ii //

i cannot
define fine,

and

i cannot
deride the ride,

yet

i cannot
describe the scribe,

but

i cannot
disguise this guise,

and

i cannot
deny the i,

because

i cannot
design the sign,

yet

i cannot
divine divine,

but

i cannot
decry the cry,

really,

i cannot
descry the why.

on individuality //

never have
i seen a
flower
quite like
your bloom.

on infrastructure //

build a bridge
in your mind,
not a wall.

on inspiration //

she smiled
at the eternal
waves that licked
her feet,

and wrote
poems to them
constantly.

on instinct //

humans are
painfully
creative.

on intuition //

god would
always
speak in
native
tongue.

on itinerary //

our final
port of call
accepts
no vessels.

on judgment //

who would
we be
to tell
nature
what shapes
are lovely?

on justification //

the false
cannot
mount a
true case.

on kin //

family
is
given
and
chosen.

on kin ii //

you will
know who
you are
by how
you make
them feel.

on kindness //

real love
is freely
given

and costs
nothing
to receive.

on kisses //

nothing
rolls off
the tongue
like
another one.

on knowledge //

and in
a moment

i saw
the meaning;

the place
the patterns
are all
convening.

my heart;
my mind,

throbbing,
gleaning.

on knowledge ii //

if it is
hard to
look at,

be strong
enough
to see.

on learning //

when our
minds will
support
growth of
something new,

we are
forever
in the
flower
of youth.

on learning ii //

as a
lesson
calls
out to
you with
passion,

consider
it a
lover.

on liberation //

only a
body
can be
shackled.

on listening //

perhaps
if we
were more
understanding,

we might
feel more
understood.

communication;
common good.

on loneliness //

pride
invites
us to
set
ourselves
aside,

and in
its
isolation
dies.

on loneliness ii //

and how
deep a
wound is
the human
condition?

on loneliness iii //

a heart
is by
itself
divided.

on love //

if i
have ever
loved you,

i love
you still.

then
now
forever

and always
will.

on love ii //

how could
i ask
three
english
words
to hold
all of
what i
feel for
you?

on lovemaking //

her whole
body ached
to express
itself nakedly.

on lovers //

by
no means
must you
love me
as i am.

but
i am
as i am,

i am
the only
one of
me to
love.

on manifestation //

with our
words we
speak our
universe.

on manners //

you are
as kind
as you
can will
yourself
to be.

on meditation //

you make
as much
room for
your thoughts
as you do
silent space.

on messages //

the feeling
you send
with is
received.

on motivation //

only you
know where
your why
comes from.

on nature //

life
is by
itself
defined.

on nature ii //

maybe
death and i
are but
old friends,

meeting
each time the
mortal
coil ends?

on nature iii //

i know
the rain.

she loves me
so much,

gently
reminding
every inch

what it

is like

to be

t o u c h e d.

on neglect //

the devil
tends to
dine at
forgotten
tables.

on nights //

if i
wrote an
ode to
the sun,

it would
sound like
moonlight.

on nonsense //

love is
beyond
reason.

on nostalgia //

hold me

for a moment,

would you?

i want to
forget
where my
edges are.

on nostalgia ii //

the mind
enjoys
the sweetest
moments
at least
twice.

on now //

seamless
is the
fabric
we lie
together
in side
by side.

on now ii //

actuality—
she is
the most
gorgeous
form of
reality.

virility—
above
the veil
of heady
glamour;
fertility.

royalty—
rise up
into the
crown you
wear now;
loyalty.

to yourself
to the truth
to your dreams

to the real
edges of your skin;
let feeling in.

wasting
such
abundance
would be
to deny
the incredible
vessel
the universe
dropped
you in;

the soul
within.

on obstruction //

who would
ask you
to dam
the river
of yourself?

on occupation //

every
morning
you decide
where to
place the
sunshine
of your
golden
attention—

she grows
the fruit
of your
life.

on opportunity //

the mass
of each
moment
is equal.

on opportunity ii //

life can
be so
much and
it can
be so
little.

on optimism //

make no
mistake,

i will
not rest
until
i am
in dreams
awake.

on overwhelm //

eyes on
head up
chin level . . .

it is
happening
again.

jaw set
heart open
hands steady . . .

you know
it is
happening
again.

feet sure
face soft
mind ready . . .

this time
you know
how to

feel as
it is
happening
again.

on pain //

when it
moves,
it aches
beauty.

when it
hurts,
it cries
poetry.

on pain ii //

what divides us
also unites us.

on pain iii //

she puts
on her
bravest
face,

always
meeting
the end
with grace,

but there
within
hides a
softer
space,

where her
heart bleeds
quiet
without
a trace,

alone
and held
in her
own embrace.

on passion //

i want
to feel
you
in the
tips
of your
fingers

on fire

hot
with
desire

that
heat

total
focus

is what
my
body
requires.

on partnership //

the world
feels less
divided
when our
souls are
united.

on pillowtalk //

late at night,

i can hear
our voices
in timeless
chorus,

joining those
who have
whispered love
before us.

on pillowtalk ii //

i could
have gone
to bed
with you
for an
hour or
a lifetime.

on play //

whoever
keeps
score
has lost
track of
the sport.

on pleasing //

i want
everything
about me
to make
you feel
at home.

on phones //

when did
we agree
to be
available
all of
the time?

on prayer //

she let
the sun
pour down
upon
her crown

worn as
a gown;
golden
all around.

on purpose //

aim for
what you
came for.

on quarrel //

at the table
we bit down
into the most

delicious
tension

i had ever
tasted.

. . . i went back
with my fork
for more.

on quarrel ii //

you may
strike me
in the breast;

you lay
the blow
upon your chest.

i open
my heart
in full protest.

on quarrel iii //

love and pain
lie so close
together
late at night.

on rationalization //

will we let
our feelings
justify
our failings?

on realization //

those things
you see
reflected
in another
are yours
to keep.

on refinement //

my favorite
ideas live
free of
final form.

on reflection //

i see
better in
your eyes.

that glass
on the wall?

only
a mirror
by disguise.

on release //

i caught love

last night

like a
lightning bug;

she flew
into my jar

and lit it up

from the
inside.

so then,

i let
her go
into the dark.

on repair //

all things
tend to heal
when we let
them be.

on rescue //

i am the only one
who will come
to save me:

i am the sailor,
the storm, the eye,
and the sea.

on resilience //

no man is
made in his
finest hour.

on revenge //

anger
is a
poison
we choose
to drink.

on safety //

true love
has no
condition
to speak of.

on satisfaction //

nothing
tastes
as sweet
as juice
squeezed
of your
effort.

on satisfaction ii //

i give you
permission
to enjoy
anything
you want.

on schoolmates //

we used to
pass notes,

to fold slips
of paper;

time and
space so
carefully
arranged
to express
our love.

on self-concept //

never shrink
to fit into
the box of
who they
think you are.

on self-control //

the power
we fear most
is our own.

on self-control ii //

each time
i hold
my forked
tongue
i have won.

on self-sabotage //

stop it
or it
stops you.

on service //

do it
because
it is
yours
to do.

on sides //

but only
he with eyes
to see both
can choose one.

on sleepovers //

i feel
high as
the sky
above,

so much!
so real!

so drunk
in love.

i fly
inside;
a singing
dove.

on soul //

you come like
the dawn of god
in a pagan sky.
rising like a
long-needed tide, while
engulfing my parched planet in
the blue flood that
you are;
coloring the black-and-white
world,
with shades of human violet. so
vivid they burn like
warm water
on a frozen hand.
reaching for eternity yet
holding on to its
morality
saying
i can
never
let
her
go.

on soul ii //

there is
a voice
you can
not mute
when it
speaks
truth
to you.

on spirit //

i can feel
your ghost
from my crown
to my toes . . .

shivers
claiming
every inch
through which
it flows.

on spontaneity //

life is an
improvisational art,

going off script
right from the start.

on suffering //

open your eyes!

see your grief
is your love
disguised.

on teaching //

you are
a candle

as you
illuminate
a room.

on tenacity //

if we were
going to
give up,

we would have.

on tenacity ii //

faith is
stronger
than pain
makes
weak.

on transformation //

i see
your
innocence,

and i
raise you
wisdom.

on truth //

speak if
it need
be said
out loud.

on truth ii //

if you
do not
say it,

maybe
no one
else will.

on uncertainty //

my heart
beats like
the end
of a
question
mark;

pounding,
asking,
in the dark.

on unity //

i gaze
into
both of
your eyes
seeing
oneness
as it
comes
in two.

on unity ii //

why would
life not be
sacred
in all of
its forms?

on unity iii //

i love
when we
slip out
of time
and space

into
that holy
place

where the
giver
and the
receiver
are one;

separateness
undone.

on utopia //

perfect
is an
imagined
state of mind.

on voice //

you are

yourself

best
expressed.

on voice ii //

your life
is the sort
of poem
that you write
it as.

on voice iii //

god did
not mean
for your
lips to
stay shut.

on wisdom //

the place
where the
heart breaks
knows the
difference.

on wisdom ii //

on the
wings
of your
fall
comes
your flight.

on wisdom iii //

always
growth through
what you
go through.

on wisdom iv //

those truly
clever
know they
can ever
do better.

on wit //

know when your
arrow lands it
pierces the skin.

on wives //

remember
to take care
of your muse—

do not
nature's
beauty
abuse.

on woman //

she felt
her body,

like a
violin;

its music,
vibration

conducted
from within.

on woman ii //

she was

symphony;
reverie

naked;
sacred

spiritual;
miracle

and she
said it
out loud!

on woman iii //

i am
a living
masterpiece

for the
young
artist

with
eyes
to see

he is
a lord
in heaven

if he
chooses
to be.

my love,
my life;

your majesty.

i am
a kingmaker;

a queen.

on words //

when the
tongue slips
the heart falls.

on words ii //

it is
your lips
that speak
the shift;

that sink,

that lift.

on words iii //

the waves
of your
voice break
on the
shores of
someone.

on words iv //

her words
could not
possibly
contain
her joy!

on words v //

what i
can write
falls
at the
feet of
what i
can feel.

on worship //

some
heartbroken
masses
hope in
churches,

waiting to
be saved.

but
you and i
share a
glass
of wine;

drinking to
the break
and the
mend,

the same.

on writing //

when you
yoke her
with a
golden thread,

english is
a chariot.

on writing ii //

she spoke.

so clear
and sweet
the sounds . . .

her word
resounds,

her joy
abounds,

her path
confounds,

her heart
rebounds,

her soul
surrounds,

her life
astounds,

her being
grounds.

La Reunion Publishing is an imprint of Deep Vellum established in 2019 to share the stories of the people and places of Texas. La Reunion is named after the utopian socialist colony founded by Frenchman Victor Considerant on the west bank of the Trinity River across from the then-fledgling town of Dallas in 1855. Considerant considered Texas as the promised land: a land of unbridled and unparalleled opportunity, with its story yet to be written, and the La Reunion settlers added an international mindset and pioneering spirit that is still reflected in Dallas, and across Texas, today. La Reunion publishes books that explore the story of Texas from all sides, critically engaging with the myths, histories, and the untold stories that make Texas the land of literature come to life.